THE GOOD SHEPHERD'S *PASTURE*

A STORY OF YOUR BAPTISM

Written by
ELIZABETH HARWELL

Illustrated by
LAURA PENNEBAKER

cdm
DISCIPLESHIP MINISTRIES

Published by:
Committee on Discipleship Ministries
1700 North Brown Road, Suite 102
Lawrenceville, Georgia 30043
800-283-1357 / 678-825-1100
www.pcacdm.org

ISBN: 13:978-1-944964-39-9

FOREWORD

AS A PASTOR AND A FATHER, I'm profoundly grateful for Elizabeth Harwell's labor of love. When her husband, Andrew, shared *The Good Shepherd's Pasture* with me, I felt I was reading an answer to prayer, a book that verbalized what my heart longed for but had not the words to express: the beauty of growing up as a child of the covenant, one baptized in the name of the Father and of the Son and of the Holy Spirit. This book is a gift for two reasons. First, Elizabeth offers us a vivid picture of life in the covenant family and the blessings it entails. Using the image of the Good Pasture as an analogy for the visible church, she opens the door wide for our children to taste and see the goodness of our Shepherd Jesus and to hear the siren song of love He sings through the sign of the thing signified, baptism. As a father who longs for his little girls to know the grace of Jesus proclaimed in their baptisms, this will be a book I return to with them again and again.

Second, she invites not only our children, but parents as well to remember our baptisms. To come back to the water and bathe afresh in the grace of the gospel. To remember that when we stumble, the promise of forgiveness through the blood of Jesus cries out to us from the water that fell from our pastor's hands. That when we feel alone and abandoned, there is a Shepherd who has called us by name, claimed us as His own, and will not let us go. That when we hear the siren songs of other pastures, we would recall again the better song of Jesus proclaimed in the baptismal fount and follow Him instead. That when we feel proud, the sight of infants carried by their parents to receive the sign of grace would remind us all how we came to Jesus in the first place: not as self-sufficient men and women, but as little children dependent upon Him alone.

Take and read. Jesus beckons. May your baptisms be a means of grace for you till you see Jesus face to face.

CALEB CLICK / YOUNG ADULT PASTOR / PERIMETER CHURCH / ATLANTA, GA

LET ME TELL you a story, Little One. Can you imagine a pasture full of sheep? We are very much like them.

YES, LIKE SHEEP! Sheep need a shepherd. A shepherd is someone who takes care of sheep: leading them to the right food to eat, guiding them away from danger, and making sure they have everything they need.

When sheep don't have a shepherd, they do silly things like eat grass that makes them sick or wander off into dangerous places. We can be a lot like sheep.

JESUS IS OUR GOOD Shepherd. He takes care of His children like a shepherd would take care of his sheep. And yet, there was a time when we tried to live our life without a shepherd. There was a time when we actually tried to be our own shepherd. This was not only dangerous, but also terribly wrong. We were telling God—using our mouth that He made, with the breath that He breathed into us—that we didn't need Him.

God had to punish this sin of our trying to be our own shepherd. It was the only way He could truly love the world—by freeing us up from trying to rescue ourselves. Any of us would (and do) hide from God's anger over sin.

But our Shepherd, Jesus, is not like anyone else. He did not run. He laid down His life for His sheep. He took the punishment He did not deserve. Yes, for the sheep who said they didn't need Him!

AND WHILE WE WERE still wandering away from Him, the Good Shepherd called us by name and opened the gate to His pasture. Our name had never sounded so right before. It was being spoken by the One who knew our name even before our parents did!

His call ran through our hearts and into our feet, and we dropped everything to be with Him. We were at home with Jesus.

NOW WE, AS THE Good
Shepherd's sheep, live here
in His pasture.

WE ARE EATING THE good grass and drinking the good water and being taken care of by Jesus Himself, who knows all of the things that we need even before we can tell Him.

AND THERE ARE OTHERS in this pasture, too. Some we know, and some we have never met! Sheep carry a mark on their wool to show to whom they belong—a sign of their Shepherd. All of us here in this pasture carry a sign, too. Our baptism is the mark of our Shepherd, Jesus. Do you know why you were baptized?

LONG AGO, BEFORE JESUS CAME, God commanded that men and their sons be marked, showing that the people in their homes served the true God. It was meant to be a sign—a story pointing to Jesus, who would one day come and die for all His sheep. Jesus would make a promise with His blood that those who belonged to Him would *always* belong to Him.

And, He did come! He took the punishment we deserved, and He also lived His life exactly the way God asks us to live. He had a perfectly clean heart, never dirty with wrong—no lying or taking what wasn't His, not even a mean thought! Because Jesus is God's Son—and because He rose to life after His death—He can wash our hearts clean, too.

ON THE WONDERFUL DAY THAT you were baptized, our pastor poured water over you as a sign of what Jesus can do in your heart. He can take your heart and our hearts that want to do wrong, and He can make them new. He can give us hearts that want to obey Him. He can give you a heart that *wants* a shepherd instead of wanting to be its own shepherd.

Baptism is a sign that points us to Jesus and a mark that we belong to His church. On the day you were baptized, we were telling the world around us that you live in a home that follows the Good Shepherd, and we were telling you that you are not an outsider. You belong in this pasture with us.

OH, LITTLE ONE, what a gift that you get to grow up in the good pasture with us! You may not see Jesus as your Shepherd yet, but He walks with us daily. He is taking care of our family.

WHEN WE TUCK YOU into bed, His hand is over ours. When there is food on your dinner plate, it has come by His loving care. When you cry big tears onto our shoulders, He is holding you, too. Even our laughter is an echo of *His* joy!

ONE DAY, YOU MAY decide to wander outside of this pasture and see what the grass looks like in other places, but I hope you don't ever have to know what life is like without the Shepherd. We pray that you will grow up in wonder of our promise-keeping Jesus, and you will stay because you have seen that He is good.

IN A TIME TO COME, perhaps
even today, the Shepherd will call out
your name. Imagine—the One who breathed
you into life calling out to you, reaching out
His hand for you to walk with Him forever.
We pray you drop everything and run to Him.
Your heart will find its truest home
as He sweeps you up into
His arms.

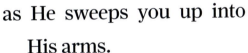

FOR NOW, SIT ON our laps and listen to us tell love stories about the Good Shepherd and know that His love and His promises are for you, too.

He is bringing other sheep into the pasture. Watch with us in wonder as He is creating a family from all sorts of people. Listen closely to hear them all shouting of the goodness of the Shepherd who loves them, too!

LAY YOUR HEAD DOWN AND rest with us in the pasture of the Good Shepherd. As you play, and run, and walk with us through life, listen for Jesus singing love songs over our family. If you cannot hear Him yet, we will sing back His words over you.

WE WILL KEEP SINGING until, one day, you hear His voice rising above our voices. We will watch the delight on your face as you repeat the love song you hear. And then, Little One, run with remembrance. Remember the promises you were given at your baptism: Jesus knows you and He loves you.

Let those promises wash over you like the water off the pastor's hands! And then run with the song to those who haven't heard about our Shepherd. Sing the songs of the good pasture and of the Good Shepherd who knows and loves His sheep.

"AND SURELY GOODNESS AND
MERCY WILL FOLLOW YOU ALL
THE DAYS OF YOUR LIFE."

ELIZABETH HARWELL is the wife of a pastor, the introverted mother of three extroverts (Wilson, Charlie, and Rosemary) and a lover of words. She and her husband Andrew spent the first ten years of their marriage on staff with a campus ministry (at Auburn University and then at the University of Southern Mississippi), and now are pivoting from campus ministry to pastoring in a local church. When not writing, she can be found hiding in the pantry with a dark chocolate bar, therapeutically cleaning house, or trying to read poetry to her children whilst they pelt her with NERF gun bullets.

LAURA PENNEBAKER is an oil and watercolor artist. Laura graduated with a Bachelor of Fine Arts degree from the University of Mississippi in 2001. She enjoys painting with a colorful palette and a loose brushstroke. This is her first book to illustrate. Laura lives in Hattiesburg, MS with her husband and three children.